Alexei and the Firebird

by Tony Bradman
Illustrated by Victoria Assanelli

OXFORD
UNIVERSITY PRESS

Chapter 1
The apple thief

Long ago in Russia, there was a rich lord who lived in a very grand house. Outside his house there was an apple orchard with a very special tree ... a tree that bore apples of pure gold. The apples hung gleaming and glistening on the branches, and every year the lord looked forward to his golden harvest.

However, one autumn, somebody got there before him.

The largest golden apple had been stolen.

"We need to make sure the thief doesn't steal any more of my golden apples," the lord said angrily. "Who will stay in the orchard tonight and keep watch?"

None of the servants wanted to keep watch. They all looked at Alexei. He was the youngest.

Alexei rolled his eyes. "Oh, very well," he said. "I'll do it."

That night, as the sun went down, Alexei sat at the foot of the special tree and waited. As darkness wrapped round him, he became <u>aware</u> of every little noise: leaves rustling, mice scuffling, bats squeaking.

Although he felt nervous, after a while Alexei's eyes began to grow heavy.

To be <u>aware</u> of something is to realize it is there. Think about your surroundings at the moment. What sights or sounds are you <u>aware</u> of?

Alexei woke suddenly when he heard the sound of beating wings.

He gazed in wonder as a strange bird flew into the orchard. It glowed with a red and orange light, as if it was on fire. The bird swooped down and plucked a golden apple with its beak.

Alexei jumped up to stop it, but the bird flew away. A single fiery-red feather drifted to the ground.

When Alexei gazed at the bird, did he look at it quickly or did he stare at it for a long time? Can you gaze at something in the room?

Chapter 2
Waiting for the firebird

In the morning, Alexei told the lord what had happened and showed him the feather. It still glowed like a flame.

"Only one bird has feathers like that," said the lord, in amazement. "The firebird."

The other servants gasped. They had heard of the firebird from old legends. There were many stories about its power and beauty.

"Maybe somebody is *sending* it here to steal your golden apples, Lord," suggested Alexei.

"We must find out who," said the lord. "Someone will have to keep watch in the orchard again tonight, then follow the firebird wherever it goes."

The other servants didn't hesitate. They all turned to look at Alexei.

He rolled his eyes. "I'll do it."

The servants didn't hesitate before looking at Alexei. Does that mean they acted quickly or waited a while?

That night, Alexei sat at the foot of the tree with the firebird's feather tucked in his belt. This time he was determined to stay awake.

When the night was at its darkest point, he heard the sound of beating wings. Soon the firebird flew into view, its fiery glow lighting up the night sky.

Alexei watched as the firebird grabbed another golden apple in its beak, then flew off.

Alexei set off after the firebird. He had to be fast to keep up with it, as it glided over fields and past sleeping villages. Luckily he was fit from running up and down the stairs in the lord's house.

Eventually, just as the sun was rising, the firebird hovered above a great palace. The palace belonged to the tsar – the ruler of all of Russia.

Chapter 3
The tsar's palace

Alexei saw the firebird land on the highest roof of the palace.

He slipped through the open gates into a courtyard full of lords, ladies and other wealthy-looking people. They seemed angry and upset.

"Why have you been sending the firebird to steal from us, Your Majesty?" yelled one of them. "Come out and tell us!"

After a while, the tsar came out on to a balcony to speak to the crowd. The lords and ladies fell silent in his presence.

"Forgive me. I had no choice but to send the firebird!" he said. "A villain has captured my daughter, Princess Vasilisa. He won't set her free unless I give him all the gold in the land."

If you are in someone's presence, you are where they are. Are there times at school when you have to be silent because of someone's presence?

"That's terrible, Your Majesty!" called out one of the lords. "Who is this villain?"

"I can hardly bring myself to say his name," said the tsar. He gripped the balcony. "It's … Koschei."

The lords gasped in horror. Even Alexei had heard of Koschei, who <u>claimed</u> to be even more powerful than the tsar himself!

Koschei <u>claimed</u> to be more powerful than the tsar. Does that mean he really was more powerful than the tsar, or just that he said he was?

"I'm happy to give you my gold if it will bring the princess back, Your Majesty," one lord said. Others called out in agreement.

"There isn't enough gold in the land to satisfy Koschei," said the tsar, with a sigh. "I need someone to go and rescue the princess."

Alexei could see none of the lords or ladies liked that idea.

"Not me!" one of the lords said, backing away.

"Koschei is terrifying!" added a lady. "Nobody could defeat him."

All the lords and ladies started talking at once. Alexei rolled his eyes. He pushed through them until he was in front of the balcony.

"Errr … excuse me, Your Majesty," he yelled at the top of his voice. "I'll do it."

The lords and ladies all turned to stare at him, then laughed.

"Silence!" shouted the tsar. The crowd immediately went quiet. "Who are you, boy?"

"My name is Alexei," he said, "and I want to help." Secretly, he was also hoping for a reward, but he didn't say so.

Alexei knew facing Koschei would be hard, but he had nothing to lose.

"Wonderful!" said the tsar, as he came down from the balcony to see Alexei. "In that case, you can set off straight away! You'll need some armour and a sword."

"No, thanks," said Alexei. He wasn't used to being weighed down with heavy armour, and he didn't think he could <u>control</u> a sword. He would rely on his wits.

Why might Alexei think that he wouldn't be able to <u>control</u> a sword?

"Very well," said the tsar. "The firebird can show you the way to Koschei's castle."

The firebird took off from the roof of the castle and landed beside Alexei, who climbed on to its back.

The tsar and the lords and ladies waved them goodbye as the firebird took off.

Chapter 4
Koschei's castle

The firebird flew over fields and mountains. Alexei peered down at a dark, gloomy forest.

"I'm glad I don't have to walk through there," he said to himself, looking down at the trees below.

At last, the firebird landed on a hill. Alexei slid from its back and looked down at Koschei's castle. His heart sank.

The castle's walls were tall and grim. There were thick gates with sharp spikes and a moat full of dark, dank water.

"Maybe this wasn't such a good idea," said Alexei. Just then, the firebird beat its wings and flew off.

Alexei took the firebird's feather from his belt, where he'd tucked it, and held it for courage. He took a deep breath. Then he set off down the hill and found a path that led to the castle gates.

The guards took him to Koschei, who was waiting in a cavernous hall. Koschei was tall and grim, just like the walls of his castle. He scowled, and Alexei felt a chill run down his spine.

"I saw the firebird, so I know the tsar has sent you," snapped Koschei. "I hope you've come to tell me when he will be sending me more gold."

"Sorry, I'm afraid you won't be getting any more gold," said Alexei. "I've come to make you set Princess Vasilisa free."

Koschei stared at him for a moment, then burst out laughing. "That's the funniest thing I've ever heard!" said Koschei at last. "Throw him in the dungeon with the princess."

"That could have gone better," thought Alexei.

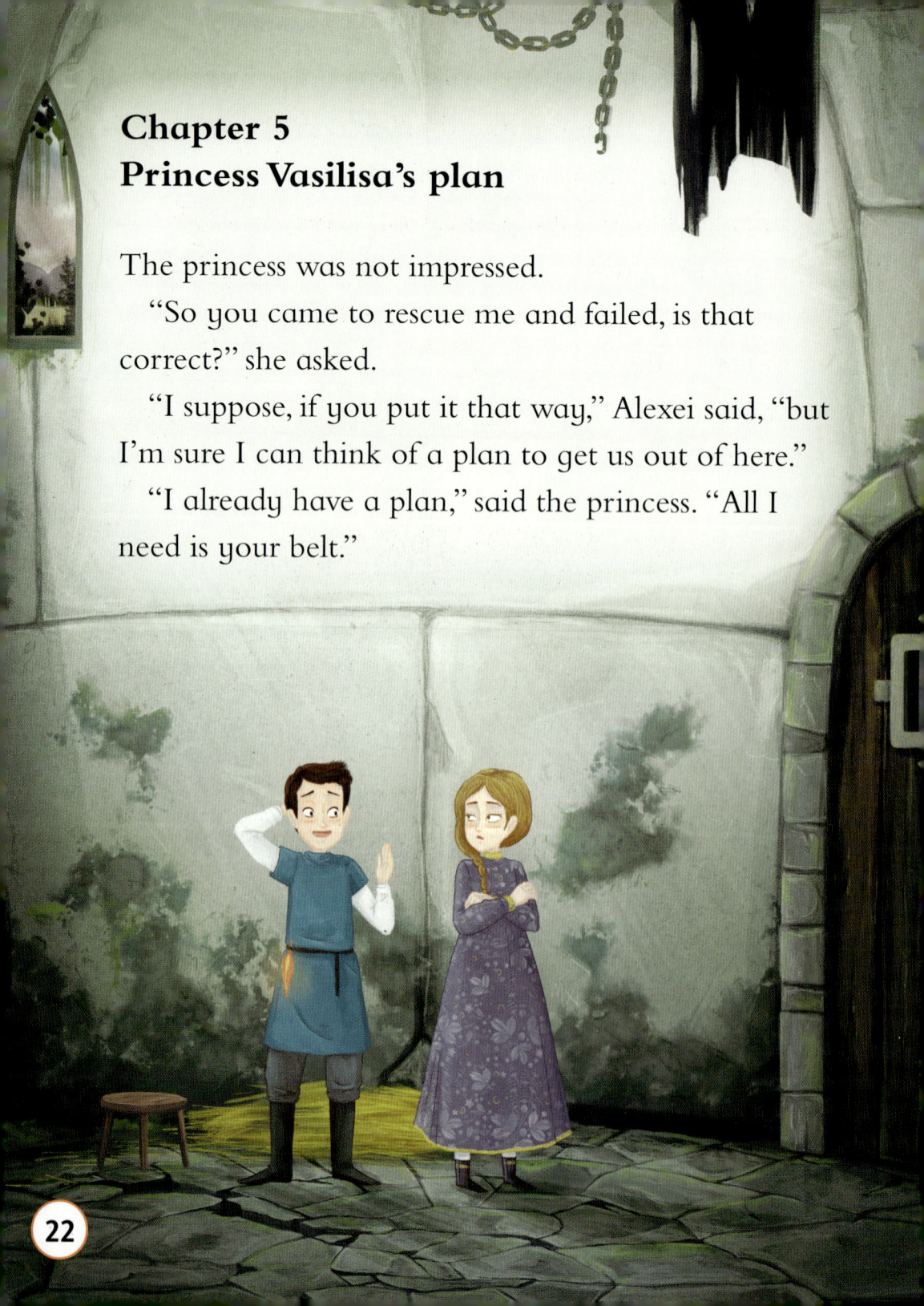

Chapter 5
Princess Vasilisa's plan

The princess was not impressed.

"So you came to rescue me and failed, is that correct?" she asked.

"I suppose, if you put it that way," Alexei said, "but I'm sure I can think of a plan to get us out of here."

"I already have a plan," said the princess. "All I need is your belt."

They waited until the guard fell asleep.

Then the princess used her hairpin and Alexei's belt, like a fishing line, to get the key from the guard.

A few minutes later they were sneaking out of the castle.

"This is really going to <u>ruin</u> Koschei's day," the princess whispered.

> Why did the princess think that sneaking out of the castle would <u>ruin</u> Koschei's day? Can you think of another word that could be used instead of '<u>ruin</u>'?

Unfortunately, a guard on the castle walls spotted them as they slipped out through a side door. "The prisoners are escaping!" he yelled.

"Run for it!" shouted the princess. She shot off, and Alexei had to sprint to keep up with her.

Behind them came the thunder of hooves. Alexei turned to see Koschei and his guards charging after them on horseback.

"You won't get away from me!" yelled Koschei.

The princess and Alexei ran faster. They had two options: to go up the hill or into the dark, gloomy forest.

"He's bound to catch us if we stay out in the open!" said Alexei, panting hard.

"Let's go this way then," yelled the princess.

They ran towards the trees.

Koschei and his guards galloped after them.

Alexei and the princess followed the twisting, turning paths through the trees, but the thundering sound of hooves kept getting louder.

Just in time, the princess grabbed Alexei's arm, and they dived behind a fallen tree. Koschei and his guards galloped past and vanished in among the trees.

"Phew, they've gone," said Alexei.

"That only leaves one problem," said the princess. "We're lost."

Alexei realized she was right. It was so dark they couldn't see which direction they'd come in. Suddenly, Alexei remembered the firebird's feather. He reached down to his belt and pulled it out. Like a glowing candle, it lit their way.

After a while they reached a clearing. A blazing light became visible in the sky. It was the firebird.

What helped make the firebird visible in the dark sky?

Chapter 6
Firebird to the rescue

The firebird landed in the clearing.

"Hello, old friend," said Alexei, stroking it on the neck. The firebird seemed to glow even brighter with pleasure.

Alexei and the princess climbed on its back. It rose into the air and quickly transported them back to the tsar's palace.

The tsar and the lords and ladies were astonished when the princess and Alexei landed in the palace courtyard. Everyone was delighted, of course. The tsar was happy because his daughter was free again. The lords and ladies were happy because the tsar said he would give them back everything the firebird had stolen.

Alexei was happy too, because the tsar promised to give him all the gold he could wish for.

Alexei bought some land from his old lord and built a large house.

Soon he had plenty of his own servants. He was a good lord, and they all liked him – mostly because he didn't make them run up and down the stairs all the time.

The princess would often come to see Alexei. The firebird sometimes paid them a visit, too.

As for Koschei and his guards … well, it seems they never came out of the dark, gloomy forest. Nobody ever saw them again.

Read and discuss

Read and talk about the following questions.

Page 4: Why do you think Alexei was more aware of the noises around him, as he sat in the orchard at night, than he might normally be?

Page 5: When you gaze at something, do you look at it for a long or short time?

Page 7: Can you think of a word that could be used instead of 'hesitate'?

Page 11: Why do you think the tsar's presence made everyone fall silent?

Page 12: Can you think of anything else that Koschei might claim about himself?

Page 16: How might Alexei have controlled the firebird when he rode on its back?

Page 23: Do you think that Koschei's day was ruined? Why?/Why not?

Page 27: What prefix do we add to the word 'visible' to make a word with the opposite meaning?